MW01109880

The Mission of Sorrow

On God's Benevolent Design in our Afflictions

by Gardiner Spring

Originally published in 1863.

CONTENTS:

SORROW– GOD'S WITNESS

It must be a hard heart that is not touched with the sorrows of the bereaved. Our sympathy may give courage to the mourner, and relieve his solitude, even where it cannot alleviate his woes. Calamity in every form makes an appeal to every Christian mind for correspondent feeling, for fellowship, for counsel. The sorrows which for months past have inundated this land, and which now sweep over it like the waves of the sea, have been vividly present to the writer of these pages; and he would gladly give utterance to a few thoughts in which his own heart beats in unison with the afflicted. We weep with those who weep. "A friend loves at all times, and a brother is born for adversity." We "remember those who are in adversity, as being ourselves also in the body." We have all much to be thankful for, and much to mourn over. Sorrow has its approved mission. If the Father of mercies "does not afflict willingly, nor grieve the children of men," there must be some reason for these afflictions– a "needs be" that is absolute and imperative. We should "hear the rod, and him who has appointed it."

Atheism is the great vice of the human mind. It is the nature of sin to be blindfold, especially to the existence and attributes and presence of the great Unseen. It is the element of sin to live at a distance from God. It is the refuge and triumph of sin, when "the fool has said in his heart, There is no God."

"The owlet Atheism,
Sailing on obscene wings across the noon,
Drops his blue-fringed lids, and shuts them close,
And hooting at the glorious sun in heaven,
Cries out, Where is it?"

There is no more emphatic or terse description of wicked men than that they are "without God in the world." This is their character, and leads to all their negligence, all their unbelief, and all the varied forms of their ungodliness. When once a man loses sight of the God of heaven, and has no abiding impressions of him "in whose hand is the soul of every living thing," who can measure or limit his roving, or tell where he will stop? Yet to this practical atheism men are everywhere exposed. The tendency to it is strong and seductive, and impelled by all the subtlety of him "who goes about like a roaring lion, seeking whom he may devour."

Men live and go forth into the world, and look on its beauty and its bloom, every planet and star reflecting the image of the Deity, every stream and summer cloud and breathing fragrance all with one voice vocal with his praise; yet they are ignorant of God, estranged from God, alienated from God. What they are taught concerning him, they do not understand; what they understand, they misinterpret; what they do not misinterpret, they forget, and choose to forget, because they "do not like to retain God in their knowledge." The language of their hearts is, "Depart from us; for we desire not the knowledge of your ways." They have no notion of being controlled by "a Power above them," but rather shake off all impressions of religious obligation, that they may sin without restraint and without remorse.

It is a great thought to enter the mind that THERE IS A GOD. The knowledge of God lies at the foundation of all knowledge, of all truth, all morality, all religion, all real and permanent happiness. "This is life eternal, that they might know you, the only true God, and Jesus Christ whom you have sent."

Just as the whole frame of the universe would totter to its foundation if there were no God, so all sense of moral obligation and all true religion have nothing to rest upon where God is not known. Men must be made to think of God, to see him in some measure as he is, guiding, directing, and governing all things after the counsel of his own will. They may not stop their ears when he speaks, nor flee from his presence when he comes near; rather must they acquaint themselves with him as a God at hand, and not a God afar off, and as a very present help in the time of trouble. And this is THE MISSION OF SORROW. It is God's witness. It speaks for God to this thoughtless and suffering world.

Among the methods pursued in order to set this great and good Being before the minds of men, the Scriptures often advert to the afflictive dispensations of his providence. "The Lord is known by the judgments which he executes." This is one of the laws of his kingdom. Severe judgments indicate his being, his presence, his displeasure. They testify to his agency in all the affairs of men, and trace them to the great First Cause. A truly devout mind, one would judge, finds some repose here. It is cold comfort to be told that "man is born to trouble as the sparks fly upward," and that it is the law of his being that he must be a sufferer. Yet so it is. It is not more a law of nature that bodies lighter than the atmosphere ascend, and those that are heavier descend towards the earth, than it is the law of his being that he must be a sufferer. Every man knows this; but he would know more. And he may know more. The laws of nature are not fortuitous arrangements, but form the principles on which the God of nature conducts his wise and benevolent procedures throughout the physical creation.

It is our joy to know that there is no such thing as chance in the kingdom of nature. Everything is the result of design, and indicates the all-wise Designer. And is it less so in the moral world, and in the kingdom of grace? It would be a revolting thought that the sorrows, either of good or bad men, are uncaused, undirected, and that no all-seeing eye watches over them, and no unwearied arm restrains and controls them; and that while there is a wise and sovereign Arbiter, who balances the clouds and prepares rain for the earth, and makes the grass to grow upon the mountains, who silences the storm, and says to the invader, "hitherto shall you come, and no further," there is no such wise and benevolent supremacy over the thousand ills that flesh is heir to. Human life would be scarcely worth enjoying if blind fate were the controller. The more thoughtful and virtuous would reason as some of the wiser heathen reasoned, when, in their attempts to strike the balance between the good and the ill of man's existence, they were driven to the conclusion that it is a doubtful question whether existence is a blessing or a curse.

It is well that the Scriptures put this whole subject at rest, and explicitly instruct us, that whatever the form or degree of suffering in our world, it is the visitation of God. Sickness and poverty, drought and pestilence, disarrangement and perplexity, bereavement and death– no matter what the trial, "affliction comes not forth of the dust, neither does trouble spring out of the ground." "Shall there be evil in the city, and the Lord has not done it?" Be the means what they may, and the subordinate agents what they may– be they the sword of the enemy, or the sirocco of the desert; be they flood or fire; be they man's malignity or his envenomed tongue, the hand of God is in all.

It is not always that we realize this great truth. We stop at second causes; yet second causes are but his messengers and do his bidding. And though there are sufferings so fearful that we almost hesitate at attributing them to his providence, yet is the responsibility of directing them, one which he everywhere assumes, and which he well knows how to sustain and defend. We may never know all the reasons for these dark dispensations, until the curtain is drawn aside and lets in upon them the stronger light of eternity. It is enough to know that, though they are the darker expressions of his nature we here behold, and behold with mingled awe and reverence, behind the cloud is the pure Spirit of the full-orbed Deity.

The bereaved may indeed, under severe bereavements, lose sight of the Sovereign Dispenser. They may grieve the Holy Spirit, and take refuge in some comfortless error, and be submerged in darkness and doubt, and sink in despondency and gloom. But this is not the fitting tendency of their afflictions. When the Lord of heaven and earth thus comes out of his place to judge his enemies or chastise his friends, he sets himself directly before their minds. When he poured his wrath on Egypt, and overthrew Pharaoh and his host in the Red sea, it was that "his name might be declared throughout all the earth." When the Destroyer cut off one hundred and eighty-five thousand of the enemies of Israel in a single night, it was to teach Israel and their enemies, that God himself was in the midst of them. When the angel of the Lord smote Herod Agrippa, and he was eaten by worms; when the proud Roman boasted that there was no other God but his sword, and he and his were consumed by lightning from heaven; when the atheist monarch of Assyria affected divine honors, and in despair set fire to his palace and buried himself– in its ruins; when Nebuchadnezzar, for his presumptuous contempt of the

Most High, was driven from among men to herd with the beasts of the field and eat grass like oxen; and when Judas went and hanged himself– these and events like these announce the judicial, the executive Deity.

Any one who reads the prophecy of Ezekiel with care, cannot but notice the reason there given for the desolating judgments spoken of in that prophecy. And what is it? More than seventy times, if I mistake not, it is given in the following words– "THAT MEN MAY KNOW THAT I AM THE LORD IN THE MIDST OF THE EARTH." It has been well said that "God is in history;" and what lesson does the history of the world and the church inculcate, if not this, that "verily there is a God who judges in the earth?"

Men are not apt to stop at second causes, and overlook the great First Cause, when a resistless providence throws them into the furnace. The foundations of their skepticism then give way. Atheism itself is constrained to confess that there is a God in heaven. It is no earthly voice that speaks then. And it falls in the admonitory tones, "See now, that I, even I am he, and there is no strange God with me. I kill, and I make alive; I wound, and I heal– neither is there any that can deliver out of my hand."

This is a lesson the mourner needs to learn. It is God himself who has smitten you, my afflicted friend. It becomes you to say with one of old, "I was dumb; I opened not my mouth, because You did it." I repeat it, it was God himself, and not another, who struck the blow. And he meant to do it. "Behold, he takes away. Who can hinder him; who shall say unto him, What do you?"

'Tis God who lifts our comforts high,
Or sinks them in the grave:
He gives, and blessed be his name,
He takes but what he gave.

He had a higher claim upon the departed than your fond affection can urge. The beloved one was not yours, but his– his creature, his property, created by him, cared for by him. And has he not a right to do what he will with his own? He has not taken away more than belongs to him, nor anything which he encouraged you to believe you should long enjoy. Your rights are limited and overruled by his. It is not willingly that he afflicts, yet wisely. The season of affliction is one he employs for high and holy purposes, and for nothing more high and holy than that men may know that he exists and governs, and is the Rewarder. When he "bows his heavens and comes down, and darkness is under his feet," it is that men may know that "there is the hiding of his power."

And not infrequently, at such seasons, there are thoughts and views which so fill and absorb the mind, that God the Infinite One shuts out every other object. He has access to the mourners, and of set purpose places them in circumstances well fitted to lead them to see and acknowledge his hand. They are seasonable and well-timed instructions, and not infrequently more effective and profitable than all other teaching, and constrain them to exclaim, "Who teaches like him!"

From blank atheism I know the mind starts back with horror; yet what multitudes are satisfied with a cold and speculative belief of the Divine existence, until they feel the weight of his resistless and invisible hand. It is not the name of God merely that constitutes the Deity, but those attributes and prerogatives which are inseparable from his existence, and of which men have such faint impressions until he speaks from the thick darkness. God governs everywhere, but there are those who see him nowhere. His providence is concerned in everything, but they see it in nothing. They exclude God from his own creation. They have a God in name, but not in reality. They are "without God in the world." It is to this undutiful, ungrateful, presumptuous, and hopeless state of mind that sorrow comes to speak on God's behalf, and to remind men how much he has to do with them, and they with him. As our views of God are, so is our religion. The mere thought of God, to a mind that feels it, has more weight than all other thoughts. It is with every man either everything or nothing. It is everything to the children of sorrow.

SORROW DESERVED

One design of afflictions is to teach us that we deserve all that we suffer. No man who has a conscience will question that he is thus ill-deserving. So far from murmuring and cherishing the heart of a rebel, one would think that with the afflicted prophet he would say, "I will bear the indignation of the Lord until he pleads my cause, because I have sinned against him."

Afflictions have a moral as well as an efficient cause. God never afflicts simply because he chooses to do so. Arbitrary choice and power have no place in his government. Suffering is the sentence of justice, and not an act of sovereignty. "The curse causeless cannot come." There is no suffering where there is no sin. The reason for all the suffering in this sinful and sinning world, is the mournful fact that it is a sinful and sinning world. "Who ever perished, being innocent; or where were the righteous cut off?" The unfallen angels are not sufferers. So long as the fallen remained sinless, they were not sufferers. When this planet on which we dwell came from the hands of its Maker, it was a happy, because it was a holy world. The Tempter's foot had not trodden it, nor had it been poisoned by the venom nor polluted by the slime of the old Serpent. Our first parents were created capable of sensation, thought, and volition; their every sense and faculty was but the inlet and avenue of joy. The image of him who created them had not been effaced from their pure minds, nor was it obscured or discolored. God himself was their supreme good, and they were happy. The heavens and the earth, every creature, and every object and event around them ministered to their enjoyment. The ground was not then cursed, nor was it smitten with barrenness. They were not thorns and thistles which it brought forth, nor did savage beasts roam its mountains or its plains. There was no poisonous atmosphere, nor burning sun, nor stormy wind, nor creeping pestilence, nor bloody sword. Men did not sicken and die upon it, nor had it yet entered upon its sad career of mourning and tears. Everything was fair, because it was unblemished– everything beautiful, tranquil, and joyous, until its beauty was marred, its tranquillity disturbed, and its joys infected by sin.

Then all was changed. The ground was cursed. The air was cursed. The streams were cursed. The very flowers and plants of Eden were cursed for man's sake. Man himself was cursed. The woman was cursed. And all their descendants are born under the curse. They inherit a fallen nature, are embryo sinners, and "go astray from the womb." The varied and complicated sorrows which now attend them from the cradle to the grave, whether they be individual domestic, social, or public, are God's visitation for their iniquity. From that hour to the present, every pang that shoots through the bosom, every tear that falls upon the pallid face of sorrow, is a token of God's displeasure against sin and against man the sinner. Sorrow teaches the lesson of unworthiness and ill desert, and conveys to the proud and haughty mind the resistless, indelible impression of personal guilt and vileness.

Such is the light in which the divine oracles represent human suffering. "By one man sin entered into the world, and death by sin; and so death has passed upon all men, for that all have sinned." The terror by night and the arrow that flies by day, the restless bed of sickness and of pain, and the pestilence that walks in darkness, are faithful monitors "When you, O Lord, rebuke man for his iniquity, you make his beauty to consume away as the moth." The empire of suffering stands abreast with the empire of sin; there never was a sufferer who was not a sinner.

It is no cause of self-gratulation when we are sufferers, that we have brought the suffering upon ourselves. Yet WE cannot plead that we are guiltless. "Your way and your doings have procured these things unto you." See now that "it is an evil thing and bitter, that you have forsaken the Lord your God." If pain invades these senses, which were formed to be the avenues of pleasure, it is because we have sinned with our eyes and ears and hands, and these senses have been our tempters. If lover and friend are put far from us, and our acquaintance into darkness, it may be because they have seduced our hearts from God. If riches take to themselves wings and fly away as an eagle towards heaven, it may be because we have made our wealth our strong city, and "said to the gold, You are my trust, and to the fine gold, You are my confidence." If our fair name has been tainted by the breath of slander, or exposed to ridicule by indiscretions of our own, it is that we may be reminded how inordinately we have been "lovers of ourselves."

These are humbling thoughts, we know; yet is it no small satisfaction to know that God does not afflict us unjustly. It would be a fearful impression to struggle with, if we had the consciousness of not deserving rebuke, or if we were so deluded as to persuade ourselves that these painful dispensations are uncalled for. I have met with more instances than one of this sort in the course of my ministry, and have ever felt that while they called for faithful instruction and reproof, they also demanded compassion and sympathy. It is a perilous position which a creature thus assumes of contending with his Maker, and has no tendency to diminish or assuage his grief. Our very dreams might cure us of this presumption– "This truth was given me in secret, as though whispered in my ear. It came in a vision at night as others slept. Fear gripped me; I trembled and shook with terror. A spirit swept past my face. Its wind sent shivers up my spine. It stopped, but I couldn't see its shape. There was a form before my eyes, and a hushed voice said, 'Can a mortal be just and upright before God? Can a person be pure before the Creator?' If God cannot trust his own angels and has charged them with folly, how much less will he trust those made of clay! Their foundation is dust, and they are crushed as easily as moths. They are alive in the morning, but by evening they are dead, gone forever without a trace." Job 4:12-20

We all confess that these are just sentiments. And they soothe the troubled heart. They charm away his grief when the sufferer thus bows before the throne, accepts the punishment of his iniquity, and ascribes righteousness to his Maker.

"Almighty power, to you we bow;
How frail are we, how glorious Thou:
No more the sons of earth shall dare
With an ETERNAL GOD compare."

Man is the creature of appetite and passion; and though the creature of reflection and conscience, he often complains of the severity of God's judgments. he says within himself, Wherefore is the heat of this great anger? What have I done to deserve a blow like this? Come now, and let us reason together. Let such a one honestly attend to his own convictions, and inquire whether he is truly awake to a just sense of his obligations as God's creature. His conscience may not be so enlightened and sensitive as to lead him to feel the burden of his sins and the full weight of a self-condemning spirit. He may never have honestly made the divine law the rule of his duty, nor seen how broad it is. He may have congratulated himself on a decent exterior, not thinking that "man looks on the outward appearance, but the Lord looks on the heart." He may have thought of his fellow-men more than he has thought of God; honored them more than he has honored God, and sought their approbation and favor more than God's.

What though you do not condemn yourself for your immorality, have you no reason to reproach yourself for your ungodliness? You may have overlooked your high privileges, and lost sight of those ends of divine love in the many and discriminating favors of a kind and gracious Providence towards you from your youth up. When you contrast God's treatment of you, with your treatment of him, you may not feel so guiltless. You have been the child of his providence, the object of his care and bounty, and what return have you made to him who has thus loaded you with his benefits? Have you valued communion with him,

and sought to enjoy his presence, or found in him and from
him that peace and those joys which the world cannot give?
Have you ever taken an honest retrospect of your own
moral history? Whence is it, if you are not marvelously
ignorant of your own character, that you thus flatter
yourself that your own unworthiness and ill-desert are not
so great as those whose sufferings are less than your own?

With such a state of mind as is often cherished by
people in affliction, it is no marvel they complain of the
rod. They do not feel that they deserve it. Oh it is a dark
state of mind– dead, torpid, unfeeling state; sensitive to
bereavement and sorrow, but insensitive to unworthiness
and ill-desert.

The burden of sin is of all burdens the heaviest; but
there is a state of mind that makes light of sin, even when
the heart stoops and bleeds under the burden of sorrow. O
son, O daughter of sorrow, look into your own heart, look
into your closet and into your Bible, and then ask
conscience whether your afflictions are not deserved.

Good men are not always faultless in this matter, but
are sometimes like a bullock unaccustomed to the yoke.
"Oh," says the venerable patriarch, "Oh that it were with
me as in months past, when the Almighty was with me, and
my children were about me; when his candle shone upon
my head, and by his light I walked through darkness. But
now you have become cruel unto me; with your strong
hand you oppose yourself against me." This was a bitter
and unjustifiable complaint; yet was it from lips that had
but a little before said, "Shall we receive good at the hand
of the Lord, and shall we not receive evil?" Complaints like
this were not the true index of Job's character; for not long
after this, and in the issue of his trials, he makes that

memorable confession, "I have heard of you by the hearing of the ear, but now my eye sees you– therefore I abhor myself, and repent in dust and ashes."

The children of God are not rebels. Even under the severest afflictions they have the consciousness of their sinful character, and of their indebtedness to his forbearing mercy; and the thought cools the febrile agitation of their heart, and bids it be still. "I am the man," says the weeping prophet in his mournful Lamentations, "that has seen afflictions by the rod of his wrath. He has led me, and brought me into darkness, and not into light. He turns his hand against me all the day; he has made my chain heavy. He has bent his bow, and set me as a mark for the arrow. He has filled me with bitterness, and made me drunken with wormwood. He has broken my teeth with gravel stones; he has covered me with ashes." Language is not easily found more vividly expressive of grief and despondency. He quailed beneath beneath the rod.

But did his pensive harp echo no cheering strain? Listen while God his Maker gave him "songs in the night." He had time for reflection, for self-inspection and prayer; and in these retrospective and introverted thoughts, mourning and gratitude, the pensiveness and confidence of piety are sweetly combined. "Remembering my affliction and my misery, the wormwood and the gall, my soul has them still in remembrance, and is humbled in me. This I recall to my mind, therefore have I hope." Nor does the triumph end here. There is the song of joy from the midst of the furnace. "It is of the Lord's mercies that we are not consumed; because his compassions fail not. They are new every morning. Great is your faithfulness." It was the light of heaven illuminating his darkness. And when he subjoins, "It is good for a man that he bear the yoke in his youth; he puts his mouth in the dust, if so be there may be hope;" and then adds, "For the Lord will not cast off forever, for though he causes grief, yet will he have compassion, according to the multitude of his mercies;" and at last affirms the great and precious truth, "for he does not afflict wittingly, nor grieve the children of men"– it is the strength of heaven, making him strong in weakness; it is the smile of heaven, chasing all gloom from his solitude and depression; it is the faithfulness of heaven, leaving upon the receding cloud "a rainbow round about the throne."

Few thoughts have a more salutary influence upon the afflicted than a sense of their own unworthiness and ill-desert, especially when they contrast their afflictions with the abounding mercies of a munificent Providence. Think of your ill-desert; count your trials, and set them side by side with your enjoyments; and then ask yourself if you have nothing left to be thankful for.

"If smiling mercy crown our lives,
Its praises shall be spread;
And we'll adore the justice too
That strikes our comforts dead."

SUBMISSION UNDER SORROW

"At the funeral of President Davies, just as the people were about to take up the coffin, his mother, an aged widow, came to take the last look of her son. She gazed intently upon him; the tears fell upon the face of the corpse as she bent over it; and then, retiring a single step as she still gazed upon him, she exclaimed, 'There lies my only son, my only earthly comfort and earthly support. But there lies the will of God, and I am satisfied.'" This was Christian submission.

Afflictions are sent as a test of this great trait of the Christian character. Rightly employed, they serve not only to bring out that character, but to produce and cultivate a satisfied state of mind. It does not consist in a stoical insensibility to trials; far from it. Natural affections were given us that we might weep ourselves, and weep with those who weep. Jesus wept at the grave of Lazarus. It does not consist in having no will of our own; but in that chastened and subdued spirit which consents that the will of God should be done rather than our own will. There is no greater conquest over a supremely selfish heart than this. Many a man submits to God's will because he cannot help it; but 'forced submission' is a contradiction. There is no acquiescence when he rebels as long as he can, and yields only because he must yield, and because God is stronger than he.

There are those also who flatter themselves that they have a submissive spirit, when they have nothing to submit to. They are satisfied with the dispensations of Providence, because everything smiles about them, and all their wishes are gratified. There is no submission in this, and no subjugation of our will to the will of God, but rather a self-complacency, and a proud gratification of our own desires. Who ever thought of submitting to that which is good? There may be thankfulness for it; there ought to be; but there is no place for submission. It is only when the plan of divine Providence countervails our own desires, arrangements, and hopes, and the bitter cup is put into our hands, that we can say, "Not my will, but Yours be done." This was the spirit of our adorable and ever blessed Master, in view of such an aggregate and combination of suffering as the world never before saw, and will never see again; and it furnishes the highest exemplification of a submissive spirit.

The only difficulty in exercising a submissive spirit is, that men naturally love themselves more than God. When the carnal mind that is enmity against God is subdued, and they love God more than themselves and more than all others, this very love to him, if in due exercise, will give the preference to his will above their own. If our wishes and our will are not so dear to us as God's, we shall have no desire to oppose his will in anything. "What pleases him pleases us." If, on the other hand, we love ourselves better than God; if we love our treasures, our fame, our power, our children, our friends more than God, we cannot say, when he smites our idols, "It is well," because we have no such attachment to the divine will as leads us to subject our will to his.

Where there is no submission to God's will, afflictions give rise to morbid insensibility, discontent, murmuring, rebellion. Where it does exist, they prove its reality and its value. When the rod of God is upon our habitation, and we can say, "It is the Lord; let him do what seems him good;" when the bitter cup passes round, and we can say, "The cup which my Father gives me, shall I not drink it?" when the burdened and afflicted soul "delights more in the will of God than in anything that will can take away," who will say that afflictions are appointed in vain? One such thought, one such holy emotion, one such act of sweet submission to the divine will, called into exercise and cultivated by trials, is worth all the bereavements it costs. It will live and grow and be perpetuated when this world and its idols and idolatrous attachments have passed away.

When Shimei cursed David, he could say, "Let him curse, for the Lord has bidden him." When the enemy fell upon the family of Job, and slew his children and servants; when the fire burnt up his possessions, and a great wind from the wilderness smote the four corners of the house, and it fell upon the young men, "Job arose and tore his mantle, and shaved his head, and fell down upon the ground and worshiped, and said, The Lord gave, and the Lord has taken away; blessed be the name of the Lord." When the two sons of Aaron were suddenly made the victims of God's displeasure, "Aaron held his peace." Amid all the bitterness of their bereavements, they were happy men. They had no distrust of God. Unlike the troubled sea, their minds were tranquil. It was enough to be able to say, "The Lord reigns; let the earth rejoice." The Holy One of Israel delights in such a state of mind as this. It is of itself bright evidence of the reality of spiritual character. It is a foretaste of the river of life which flows from under the throne of God and the Lamb. It is a blessed state of mind, and tinges with "its silver lining" the dark cloud of adversity.

Why then should the children of sorrow inwardly murmur or outwardly complain? God has taken your beloved one. And will you quarrel with God? Do you well to be angry? Oh bid this tumultuous heart be still.

"Peace all our angry passions then;
Let each rebellions sigh
Be silent at his sovereign will,
And every murmur die."

Has the God only wise acted hastily in this matter? Is it difficult for you to believe that perfect rectitude cannot do wrong, that infinite wisdom cannot err, and that infinite goodness never acts unkindly? If the Sovereign Dispenser were ignorant and unwise, if he were unreasonable and unjust, or if he were merely indifferent to the sufferer's well-being, there might be ground for complaint. But there is no such God in the universe. A being of such attributes is no God.

We all feel our bereavements, and sometimes so keenly that our confidence in God is shaken, and breaks away from its strong foundations. This is all wrong. True piety is confiding, and gives its voice for God even when he "dwells in the thick darkness." Could we perceive the reasons and motives of his conduct as they lie in his own mind, unless we are rebels, we would be satisfied. God is a Rock; his work is perfect. These painful dispensations, as we have already seen, are designed to unfold his true character. In view of them, we may well say with the apostle, "O the depth of the riches, both of the wisdom and the knowledge of God. How unsearchable are his judgments, and his ways past finding out!"

We shall know more hereafter, and see more clearly how bright his wisdom and goodness shine in these dark dispensations. We cannot grasp infinity. It is asking too much of infinite Wisdom, that he should condescend to our littleness and abjectness, and see everything as we see it.

"Lord, we are blind, poor mortals blind;
We can't behold your bright abode,
Oh, 'tis beyond a creature mind
To glance a thought half way to God."

Poor blind creatures of a day, to desire that we and ours should be in our own hands rather than in his! His hand reaches through all these checkered scenes of our earthly existence. It reaches to the chambers of sickness and the bed of death; it reaches down to the grave, and up from the grave through all the successive generations of men, and all the relations they bear to him and to one another, and to the eternity where he dwells. Such knowledge is too wonderful for us. "It is high; we cannot attain unto it." Let us not then sit in judgment on what he does, but "be still, and know that he is God."

What if he had not sent these trials upon you and yours? What if he had let you alone? Are you sure your trials would have been fewer or lighter, and your condition every way better than it now is? I say, are you sure of this? Are you sure the time will never come when you will see that it was better for you that you have been visited with the very trials at which you mourn so bitterly? Are you sure the departed one would have been as well cared for as it now is, and that you could have done as well by that beloved child as God has done? It was rightly the object of your tenderest love and most cheering hopes. Are you sure that love would not have been grieved, and those hopes disappointed? Do you know that, foreseeing the dark shadows upon its pathway, love greater than yours, and purer, has not taken it from the evil to come, and housed it from the storm? Could you say, if it had lived, that "the days of its mourning are ended;" that it shall sin no more and weep no more? Could you have introduced it into "the general assembly and church of the first-born," where the spirits of just men are made perfect, where angels are its guardians and teachers, where "the glory of God enlightens it, and the Lamb is the light thereof?"

Why, why look so intently into the grave, and never beyond it? The departed are not there. It is but the mouldering clay tenement that slumbers. The intelligent, moral, and immortal one is numbered among the millions of those ransomed ones, out of whose mouth God has perfected praise. A voice from that holy world repeats the injunction, "BE STILL, AND KNOW THAT I AM GOD." His arrangements in these bereavements may excite an idolatrous heart to complaint, and an unyielding heart to rebellion; but none but a selfish heart will complain, none but idolatrous attachments will rebel.

SORROW DISTURBS IDOLATROUS ATTACHMENTS

In one form or another, all sin is idolatry. It is a violation of the command, "You shall have no other gods BEFORE ME." It sets the creature above the Creator. It ignores the Supreme Good; and sets up some created good in his place; forsaking the Fountain of living waters, and hewing out to itself cisterns, broken cisterns that hold no water.

Apostate man all the world over does this. Though formed with capacities which nothing but God can fill, he has lost his relish for the Unseen and Eternal, and seeks his highest good in the seen and temporal. This love of the creature, no longer kept in its proper place by the predominating love of the Creator, becomes an idolatrous attachment. And it is a ruinous attachment. It is the ruin of nations, the ruin of worldly men, and but for interposing grace, it would be the ruin of Christians. Nor is there anything that has a stronger tendency to weaken and break off this idolatrous attachment than afflictive dispensations.

It is altogether too favorable an opinion of human nature to suppose that men are apt to grow better under the smiles of prosperity. History teaches nothing more emphatically than that unmingled prosperity is one of the chief sources of national and individual degeneracy. "Pride and fullness of bread" embolden wickedness, inflate insolence, become the nourishment of angry dissension, collisions of interest, and pervading corruption. The Most High once said to the nation of Israel, "I spoke unto you in your prosperity, and you said, I will not hear; this has been your manner from your youth." It was the reproach of the Jew, that the apostle Paul was constrained to say to him, "Not knowing that the goodness of God leads you to repentance." God gave this people their request, but sent leanness into their souls. It is an instructive and affecting record, that "when he slew them, then they sought him; and they returned and inquired early after God; and they remembered that God was their Rock, and the high God their Redeemer."

The nations that once figured so prominently on the page of history, Assyria, Babylon, Persia, Greece, Rome, and their far-famed cities, where emperors and statesmen and philosophers and bards and merchants and bankers filled the world with fame and folly, were swept away from the pinnacle of their wealth, and from the pomp of their power. We could not live in a world so morally corrupt as this, were it not restrained and held in awe by the divine judgments. The church of God would not be safe. There would be no protection to liberty and law, no domestic and no public security, no Sabbath and no sanctuary, were it not for those "terrible things in righteousness" by which the God of our salvation has so often arisen to plead and maintain his own cause. The overthrow of Sodom and the cities of the plain, the plagues of Egypt, the destruction of

the ancient and idolatrous Canaanites, the breaking up of
the Hebrew state and monarchy, and the dispersion of the
Jews, stand forth before the world not more certainly as
judgments upon the enemies of truth and righteousness,
than as blessings to the people of God. It is right that God
should execute judgments. The world needs them. Public
and punitive dispensations consult high interests, and
terminate in the glory of his great name.

As with nations, so it is with individuals. They need to
be taught, that in seeking their highest good on earth, they
are seeking it where it is not to be found. The supreme love
of the creature is the ruin of the soul. Not many years since,
a military officer in our land exclaimed on his bed of death,
"The world– the world has ruined me!" The experience of
millions attests the truth and importance of those teachings
of the divine oracles which instruct us that "the friendship
of the world is enmity with God," and that "no man can
serve God and mammon." From the heavens and the earth,
from the chambers of the dying and the graves of the dead,
from the unsatisfying nature of all things beneath the sun,
from the sin and pollution of a world that lies in
wickedness, from hard-hearted hate and hard-handed
oppression, from tribulation and distress in all their forms,
the admonition reaches us, "Arise and depart; for this is not
your rest, because it is polluted."

One of the most distinguished and successful
preachers of the gospel in this land once said, "Until men
have taken an everlasting leave of the world, and shut
themselves up in a convent, or in hell, the love of the world
is the principal way in which they stray from God– the
principal affection which takes the place of love to him. It
is the great road to perdition; or if the gate of hell is shut by

the grace of God, it is the great road to darkness, temptation, and distress."

The psalmist understood the gracious design of affliction when he wrote the one hundred and nineteenth psalm. "It is good for me that I have been afflicted. Before I was afflicted, I went astray; but now have I kept your word." Elsewhere he says, "I know, O Lord, that your judgments are right, and that in faithfulness you have afflicted me." It was when "he was in affliction" that the vile and bloody Manasseh "besought the Lord his God, and humbled himself greatly before the God of his fathers." The afflicted patriarch had comfort in the thought when he said, "He knows the way that I take; when he has tried me, I shall come forth as gold." "In their affliction," says another prophet, "they will seek me early."

A principal element of this day of grace is, that it is a state of trial. Under this gracious arrangement everything is bringing the character of men to the test. Instruction tries it; prosperity tries it; adversity tries it. And for the most part, the great question to be decided is, whether God's creatures love the world more than him. This probationary process goes on with different and opposite results. Some there are who become worse under affliction. God said of a portion of his revolting people, "Ephraim is joined to idols; let him alone." He instructed the prophet Amos to say to backsliding Israel, "I have given you cleanness of teeth in all your cities, and lack of bread in all your palaces; yet have you not returned unto me, says the Lord. And I have withheld the rain from you, when there were yet three months to the harvest; yet have you not returned unto me, says the Lord. I have smitten you with blasting and mildew; I have sent among you the pestilence, after the manner of Egypt; your young men have I slain with the sword; yet have you not returned unto me, says the Lord. I have overthrown some of you as God overthrew Sodom and Gomorrah, and you were as a brand plucked out of the burning; yet have you not returned unto me, says the Lord." This was fearful and stiff-necked obduracy; and where God means to subdue it, he sends other and greater judgments; and where these fail of breaking the hard heart, his patience becomes wearied, and his language is, "Why should they be stricken any more? they will revolt more and more." It is a fearful procedure when God does this, and leaves the worldling to his own heart's lusts.

But while some become worse under afflictions, some become better. Afflictions awaken the conscience of the most obdurate, restrain the wicked in their sinful courses, and in defiance of their own purposes and arrangements, arrest and detain and stop them in their downward career. Many is the man who has been kept from falling, who, without them, would have sunk deep into the eternal pit. Afflictions not only often reclaim men from courses of wickedness in which they have long indulged, but not infrequently produce the physical incapacity for pursuing them. Many a man has been laid upon a bed of sickness, or has lost a limb, or become blind or deaf or palsied, that he might be kept from wickedness which it was in his heart to perpetrate.

Could the religious history of the people of God be narrated in detail, how many of them, do you think, would attribute their first religious impressions to some sad and solemn call of divine Providence? The arrow that first pierced many an adamantine heart would be traced to disappointments they little thought of– to the poverty they dreaded, to reproach and shame, or to the grave of those they loved. God accomplishes his purposes of mercy in his own way. The purpose comprises the means as well as the end; severed from the means, there is no purpose.

Affliction is often essential to the accomplishment of God's gracious design. Multitudes never would have become Christians but for pain and bereavement and losses; and after they became Christians, never would their backsliding have been healed but for the severity of their trials. But for these paternal chastisements, they would have wandered beyond the hope of recovery. God thought of them when they did not think of him, and restored their souls and led them in paths of righteousness for his name's sake.

I have seen the benefit of afflictions, and have often wondered at the wisdom and the benevolent and gracious design which ordered and directed them.

The giddy have become thoughtful, because God smote their idols. The worldling has lost his interest in the things of time, because the hand of God has touched him. The man of congenial temperament, and social habits, and instructive and pleasant converse, loses his relish for society, and is shrouded in gloom and dumb with silence, because his heart and his hopes lie buried in the grave. Nor is this all. His conscience has been disturbed with inward pangs; and while the arrows of the Almighty stuck fast in him and were drinking up his spirit, God has turned his mourning into joy and his sad lamentations into praise.

Such is the history of many a thoughtless sinner. That young widow's heart had never found its rest in God, unless it had first been buried in her husband's grave. That daughter of mirth turned from her idols to the living God, not until she called to mind the last counsels and the parting kiss of a sainted mother, and learned that God "had chosen her in the furnace of affliction." Many a heart thus broken has thus been healed. Disciplined and discouraged by tribulation, it has found the God of heaven its refuge and strength, and reposed in him without whom the whole circle of human joys is vanity. Sorrow has driven them from the world to God. It has shown them the embittered streams, and led them to the pure Fountain. It has shown them their weakness, and taught them to take hold of him "who gives power to the faint, and to them that have no might he increases strength." And now, instead of sitting alone and keeping silence, their language is, "Come, and let us return unto the Lord– for he has torn, and he will heal us; he has smitten, and he will bind us up." The mourner is then blessed, though he walks in the midst of trouble. The agitated and trembling heart has found a refuge from the storm, a strength to the needy in his distress, "a shadow from the heat when the blast of the terrible ones is as the storm against the wall."

When sorrow comes on such an errand, the house of mourning reads the lesson that there is something to rest upon besides this perishing world, and something more sacred than the attachments which terminate on earth. The soul then forgets its misery, and remembers it as the waters that pass away. She takes her harp from the willows, and sings, "Be joyful, O earth; and break forth into singing, O mountains– for the Lord has comforted his people, and will have mercy upon his afflicted." It is a new song when the child of sorrow is thus enabled to say with the apostle, "Blessed be God, even the Father of our Lord Jesus Christ, the Father of mercies and the God of all comfort; who comforts us in all our tribulation, that we may be able to comfort those who are in any trouble, by the comfort with which we are comforted of God."

Sorrow preaches as no pulpit ever preached. If "he who converts a sinner from the error of his way shall save a soul from death and cover a multitude of sins," this forbidding messenger of mercy will have crowns of rejoicing not a few in the day of the Lord Jesus. If in taking away all the mourner has loved on earth, it has given him all that is more loved in heaven; if it has robbed him of time, to give him eternity; if it falsifies the expectations of the world, and verifies purer and brighter hopes; if when the soul had lost its way, and knew not how to return to its great object and end and chief good, sorrow comes commissioned from a world of joy "to seek and save that which is lost," it has a beneficial and deserves a welcome mission.

SORROW, THE FRIEND OF CHRISTIAN GRACES

The children of God have much to struggle with. Their vocation, high and holy as it is, has a militaristic aspect. It is a protracted conflict, in which they find it necessary not only to act on the defensive, but to be the aggressors. "We wrestle not against flesh and blood, but against principalities, against powers, against the rulers of the darkness of this world, against spiritual wickedness in high places." To the peculiarity of the conflict in the first ages of the Christian church, there ever has been and is now superadded, the ordinary and never ceasing conflict with that spirit of the world which is enmity with God.

It is not only true, as has been already intimated, that the love of the world is the ruin of worldly men, it is the besetting sin of Christians. "The lust of the flesh, the lust of the eye, and the pride of life," in some of their insinuating and multifaceted forms, are evermore ensnaring them. The best of men love the world far more than they ought. Nor are they always sensible of its depressing and secularizing power. It eclipses their faith, and limits and obscures their spiritual vision. It allures their affections from God, confuses their contemplations of the realities of eternity, and is not infrequently so entwined about their heartstrings, that they have lost the life and soul of religion, and for a time appear in no way different from other men.

In miserable and criminal concurrence with these outward exposures, there are strong tendencies, from "the sin that dwells in them," not only to insensible aberrations from the straight and narrow way, but to conscious and obvious backsliding. The enemy is subtle, and the conflict severe. "The flesh lusts against the Spirit, and the Spirit against the flesh; and these are contrary the one to the other." The under-current of inbred apostasy is strong, and so resists and mingles itself with the pure river of life, that the purer waters are like the troubled sea.

God does not mean that his own children should always remain thus undistinguished from the world that lies in wickedness. We know that "all are not Israel who are of Israel." There are tares among the wheat. And though it belongs not to men to sever the just from the unjust, and although they may grow together until the harvest, the difference between them is often disclosed before the harvest sets in. If any of those who profess to be the friends of God and followers of his Son are false to their profession, he is very apt to make their unfaithfulness and hypocrisy appear, and to place them in circumstances in which their deception shall vanish like shadows before the sun, and their deceitful profession shall stand out before the church and the world. Nor is it less true that the same dispensations of his providence which detect and bring out the hypocrisy of those who have a name that they live and are dead, disclose and discover the sincerity and truthfulness of those who have more than the form of godliness.

An intimate acquaintance with the biography of good men, among other wonders of his grace, shows that the Father of mercies usually places his true friends in circumstances which prove their Christian integrity, and invigorate and burnish their graces. By early covenant he gave them to his Son, and not one of them shall be lost, nor allowed to remain undistinguished from his recognized foes. The promise is explicit– "If his children forsake my law, and walk not in my judgments; if they break my statutes, and keep not my commandments; then will I visit their transgression with the rod, and their iniquity with stripes." He loves his Son too well to violate his covenant with him, and he loves his people too well to violate his covenant with them, and allow them to rest undisturbed in their idolatrous attachments.

He has a cure for their spiritual declension and their outward backsliding. He casts them into the furnace– he tries them as silver is tried. If the dross is massive and unyielding, he heats the furnace seven times more than it is used to be heated, until the mass melts away and is consumed. This he himself declares to be his object in these afflictive dispensations. "Behold," says he, "I will melt them and try them; for how shall I do for the daughter of my people?" When he does this, and they endure the trial, they come forth like gold seven times purified. They return to him from whom they have revolted; their graces are stronger and brighter, and shine in all the beauties of holiness. There is a meaning in their afflictions, and the more emphatic as there is a reality and depth in them when they thus give brightness to their spiritual armor, and crown their conflicts with progressive victories.

The burning arrows of temptation are ordinarily showered upon the soul of the believer during the seasons of thoughtless prosperity. These fiery darts do not often fly in the valley of Baca—desolation and sorrow quench them. Such is sorrow's mission, and such is the voice of experience, and it is but an echo from the divine oracles. "Blessed is the man," say they, "who endures trials; for when he is tried, he shall receive the crown of life. Count it all joy when you fall into diverse trials; knowing this, that the trial of your faith works patience; but let patience have her perfect work, that you may be perfect and entire, wanting nothing. Now no chastening for the present seems to be joyous, but grievous; nevertheless, afterward it yields the peaceable fruits of righteousness to those who are exercised thereby." Afterward– the ploughshare struck deep; the seed requires time to ripen.

> The bud may have a bitter taste,
> But sweet will be the flower."

It is not often that a truly Christian mind long languishes under the gloom of sorrow. Dejected it may be; but there is an exhilarating power in the truths on which God has caused him to hope. Languish it may; but there are graces within, which, like plants of righteousness shrouded in darkness, are perpetually tending towards the light, and eventually emerge into the sunlight of spiritual joy.

Not only do these spiritual consolations break up the settled gloom, but bring with them a deeper and stronger consciousness of adoption into the family of God. The mourner feels that the chastening is from the faithful hand of paternal love. Under the cheerful sunshine of prosperity, many a good man has been so absorbed and gratified in the objects of time and sense, that he had little or no religious enjoyment. His joys were elsewhere. He could not say with the rejoicing thousands of Israel, "Let those who love your name be joyful in you; shout for joy, all you that are upright in heart. Let Israel rejoice in him that made him; let the children of Zion be joyful in their King, and glory in the Holy One of Israel." Far from this. They sought him, but they could not find him. They "went forward, but he was not there; backward, but they could not see him; on the right hand where he does work, but he hid himself from them; on the left hand, but they did not behold him."

Now, since the waves of sorrow began to roll over them, they find that God alone is their refuge and strength, a very present help in trouble. He is now their satisfying portion; and though everything else is fading and dying around them, they can say with the psalmist, "The Lord lives; and blessed be my rock; and let the God of my salvation be exalted."

God may be seen and enjoyed everywhere; but it is in the dark passages of our pilgrimage, in the depths of disappointed and fond expectations, on the bed of languishing, and in the death-chambers of those we love, that the light of his countenance most cheers us. They were days of fearful solemnity and sanguinary persecution when the apostle Paul wrote his rich epistle to the Christians in Rome. Nothing but the sharpest trials gave rise to such thoughts as these– "Therefore, since we have been justified through faith, we have peace with God through our Lord Jesus Christ, through whom we have gained access by faith into this grace in which we now stand. And we rejoice in the hope of the glory of God. Not only so, but we also rejoice in our sufferings, because we know that suffering produces perseverance; perseverance, character; and character, hope. And hope does not disappoint us, because God has poured out his love into our hearts by the Holy Spirit, whom he has given us." Romans 5:1-5

Who does not see the hallowed influence of abounding trials upon his abounding faith and heaven-imparted love? Who can read the eighth chapter of this epistle without perceiving that such noble thoughts and unwavering confidence were not the offspring of a tranquil age? What writer, except one from the cliffs of the overhanging storm, or the submerged cavern, or the lions den, or the "mountain of the leopards," ever uttered the triumphant language, "Who shall separate us from the love of Christ? Shall trouble or hardship or persecution or famine or nakedness or danger or sword? No, in all these things we are more than conquerors through him who loved us. For I am convinced that neither death nor life, neither angels nor demons, neither the present nor the future, nor any powers, neither height nor depth, nor anything else in all creation, will be able to separate us from the love of God that is in Christ Jesus our Lord." Romans 8:35-39

Noble man! Sufferer signally favored! Thoughts and emotions cheaply purchased by his participation with the sufferings of his suffering Lord. How far above the 'sorrows of nature' are the 'consolations of grace'. How far superior to the depressions of nature is the triumph of faith. Afflictions are not useless when grace becomes victorious. It is a beautiful remark of Pascal's, in a letter occasioned by the death of his father, "There is no consolation but in truth. All trial is sweet in Jesus Christ. He suffered and died to sanctify death and suffering. See in the magnitude of our woes the greatness of our blessings, and let the excess of our grief be the measure of our joy."

We love to have the providence of God smile upon us, and we often murmur when it frowns, even though we have so often found that it is safer for us that it should not always smile. It is recorded of ancient Israel, that "God gave them their request, but sent leanness into their souls." This is not what the Christian desires. When God frowns upon us, we should be less anxious for exemption from the suffering, than for grace to endure it. "Grace for grace," faithful grace, abundant grace– this is what the Christian needs, what he prays for, and that which follows in the footsteps of the Destroyer.

Better, unspeakably better is it to enjoy the Divine presence and the light of his countenance, without our idols, than to have our idols without his favor. Oh, what wanderers would we be, if God did not sometimes hedge up our way with thorns. Surely it is not for lack of love to his people that he severely chastises them. David could say, "My soul cleaves unto the dust; quicken me, according to your word." God heard his prayer, and sent him penitent and sorrowing to his knees. That sweet Christian poet William Cowper could "sing of mercies and of judgments," and in strains such as angels use, and rarely in sweeter tones than when he indited the hymn, "O for a closer walk with God." Sanctified trials had taught him to say,

"The dearest idol I have known,
Whatever that idol be,
Help me to tear it from your throne,
And worship only Thee.

So shall my walk be close with God,

Calm and serene my frame;
So purer light shall mark the road
That leads me to the Lamb."

I have seen, I have felt the Christian graces wither under the burning sun of prosperity; and I have seen them "revive as the corn, and grow as the vine," when these scorching rays were intercepted by clouds. The love that prefers God to creatures; the penitence and humility that have learned to "go softly," because they have "heard the rod and him who has appointed it;" the peace that tranquilizes; the fear that fills the soul with holy reverence; the hope that looks for brighter days; the joy that "glories in tribulation," looms up under the darkest skies.

From the deepest valley of humiliation, the 'eye of faith' discovers streaks of light from the mountain of God's holiness; and though dark clouds hang over it, streams of mercy flow down through their selected and grief-worn channels, filling the soul from all the fullness of God. Well does the Father of mercies say to each of his mourners, "My son, despise not the chastening of the Lord, neither be weary of his correction. For whom the Lord loves he corrects, even as a father the son in whom he delights." His own Son, his only Son, his well-beloved Son, was "made perfect through suffering." God's ways are not as our ways, nor his thoughts as our thoughts. Blind unbelief naturally errs in its interpretations of his providence. "What son is he whom the Father chastens not?"

"Those we call wretched are a chosen band.
Amid my list of blessings infinite,
Stands this the foremost, that my heart has bled.
For all I bless you; most for the severe."

SORROW—TAKING LESSONS FROM THE BIBLE

Sorrow finds no relief from the mere teachings of human reason. The lessons of pagan philosophy, even from some of the most accomplished minds the world has known, do but make it the more bitter. A celebrated orator and statesman, who flourished more than a century before the Christian era, furnishes us an instructive illustration of this thought— Marcus Cicero was from an ancient and noble family in Italy, of superior talents and culture, of military as well as academic training, scarcely less distinguished for his philosophy than his eloquence, and rose to the highest dignities of the state with no other recommendation than his personal merits. No man in Rome enjoyed a higher degree of popular favor, and no one was more deservedly hailed as "the father and deliverer of his country." But he was a disappointed man– a man of sorrow, driven into exile, a desponding wanderer in foreign lands, his property confiscated, his family persecuted, an 'idol daughter' torn from him by death, himself beheaded by a Roman centurion, and his head and hands carried to Rome. Pagan biography may be safely challenged to furnish a purer, brighter character than that of Cicero, or a more undeserved overthrow of earthly hopes, and sudden fall from the eminence of popular favor, wealth, and power, to the depths of poverty, dependence, dishonor, and death.

It may be instructive to inquire what were the resources and what the refuge of such a man in the season of adversity. He had no Bible for his teacher, and no God to go to. He was familiar with the teachings of the schools, and all the questions which relate to the academic philosophy. He himself had written a treatise in which he discusses the opinions of the sages of antiquity respecting the chief good and chief end of man; and also large treatises devoted to the consideration of topics most essential to human happiness. And now, in the hour of trial, what is his solace, and whence his consolation? His first severe affliction was his banishment from Rome. His enemies were triumphant, and in one respect he was like the king of Israel when driven from Jerusalem. He loved Rome, and would gladly have thrown some guardian shield around her. But alas, "The heathen in his blindness, bows down to wood and stone."

"A little before his exile, he took a small statue of Minerva, which had long been reverenced in his family as a kind of family deity, carried it to the capitol, and placed it in the temple of Jupiter, under the title of Minerva, the guardian of the city." He had nothing else to cheer him when he turned his back upon his beloved Rome. It was a dark hour; they were overwhelming sorrows that invaded him; but his only refuge was a marble statue in the temple of Jupiter! Such is paganism; such are the consolations of natural religion; such was the hope of the noblest man in Rome– without the Bible.

A lacerating bereavement awaited him on his return to Rome, in the death of that remarkable and accomplished woman, his daughter Tullia. His grief was inconsolable, and his lamentations most bitter. He had no comforter. Mind and body seemed to be sinking under the burden. Vain was all his philosophy to fortify himself against this overwhelming disaster. Philosophers came from all parts to comfort him; but they could not convince him that pain and misfortune and death, are no evils. They could not wipe away his tears, nor lighten his burden. He thought and read, but found nothing to relieve his despondency. Caesar wrote to him an affectionate letter of condolence; Brutus wrote another, "so friendly and affectionate that it greatly moved him;" Servius Sulpicius also wrote another, "which is thought to be a masterpiece of the consolatory kind," and which closes with the thought, that it is "unbecoming the character and dignity of such a man as Cicero to be thus inconsolable, and that he who had borne prosperity so nobly, should bear adversity with the same moderation."

But philosophy had no drops of consolation to pour into his bitter cup. He retired to a little island on the Latian shore, there, amid woods and groves, to bury himself in solitude and tears. He lost all his cheerfulness. "In the ruin of the republic," he says, "I still had Tullia; but by this last cruel wound all the rest, which seemed to be healed, are broken out again afresh." Unrelieved by the counsels of his friends, he himself wrote his treatise– "De Consolatione," with a view to employ his mind and mitigate the anguish of his sufferings. His biographer informs us that this treatise was much read by the primitive fathers, especially Lactantius. Yet strange to say, his main consolation and the main object of the treatise was to vindicate the propriety of paying divine honors to the dead; to urge the erection of a temple to her memory, as one "now admitted into the assembly of the gods;" to gratify his fond affection, and to permit his grief to evaporate at the shrine of the departed.

Such is Paganism. Such is the state of mind in Christian lands where the truths of God have no access. I have dwelt upon it, because I do not know that human reason, unenlightened by the gospel, can prescribe any better cure for the sorrow-stricken mind.

We turn from it all to the thought of the psalmist, "You have magnified Your Word above all your name." Among the varied and accumulative proofs that the

Scriptures of the Old and New Testaments are the word of God, is its adaptation to the character of man, not only as a sinner, but as a sufferer. It not merely provides ample securities for the peace of the guilty, but abundant consolations for the comfort of the miserable. Men feel the burden of their sorrows; they struggle with it; they groan under the yoke, but find no relief. They cannot avoid it; it is upon them. They cannot combat it; it is stronger than they.

The insufficiency of natural religion is never more apparent than to the consciousness of a sufferer. A survey of the earth on which we dwell discovers so much suffering, that for all that human philosophy can teach us, it appears to be inconsistent with that infinite wisdom and goodness which direct and control the affairs of men. We see 'the spoiler' everywhere; invading the habitations of the best of men as well as the worst; blighting their hopes, resting like a heavy cloud upon the fairest portion of man's earthly heritage, multiplying his trophies in the tears of the living and amid the silence of the dead, and sometimes thrusting in his sickle as though the harvest of the earth were fully ripe.

And we cannot help inquiring, Why is this? Why, under the control of unerring wisdom and infinite goodness and almighty power—is this vast aggregate of human suffering allowed thus to accumulate? Why, rather, does it exist at all; and why should humanity groan under it a single hour?

A thinking pagan like Seneca or Cicero would naturally propose this question to himself—but he would in vain seek for a solution of the problem. His philosophy is a synopsis of doubts, of suppositions, of theories, of vague conjectures, and at the same time of deep and powerful

reasoning. Yet none of its conclusions bring peace and
consolation to the miserable. It is a sorrowful philosophy, a
melancholy philosophy—profoundly melancholy, and
profoundly sad.

> "Let all the heathen writers join
> To form one perfect book;
> Great God, if once compared with yours,
> How base their writings look."

To a struggling sufferer, depressed and broken-
hearted, the teachings of natural religion are like the
scathing winds of autumn and the cold breath of winter.
They chill the soul, and drive it back into its own dark and
hopeless dungeon. There is no Sun of righteousness there,
with healing in its wings. The highest intellectual and
moral culture of pagan lands is a stranger to the source and
author, the aim and end, of human woes. It does not meet
the exigencies of the mourner; it has no mission to "bind up
the broken-hearted."

Amid such shadows as these the light of the gospel
shines with fresh brilliancy. There heart-comforting truths
are revealed, and heart-comforting scenes portrayed.
"Blessed are those who mourn; for they shall be comforted.
As the sufferings of Christ abound in us, so our consolation
also abounds by Christ. But to the poor, O Lord, you are a
refuge from the storm. To the needy in distress, you are a
shelter from the rain and the heat. Though the fig-tree does
not blossom, and there be no fruit in the vine; the field shall
yield no food, the flocks shall be cut off from the fold, and
there be no herd in the stalls; yet will I rejoice in the Lord,
and joy in the God of my salvation. Yes, though I walk
through the valley of the shadow of death, I will fear no
evil; for your rod and your staff they comfort me. Why are

you cast down, O my soul? and why are you disturbed within me? Hope in God; for I shall yet praise him who is the health of my countenance, and my God."

Here is Bible consolation. There is not one of these precious declarations but is as the shadow of a great rock in a weary land, and as rivers of water in a dry place. Martyrs have hugged their fetters, and clanked their chains, and saluted their executioners with affectionate endearments, because light and immortality are brought to light in the gospel. The promises of God, Oh they are like the dew of heaven upon the arid and exhausted heart of the mourner; they are like the breath of heaven, and redolent with its love; they are the life of the soul, transforming its sorrows into joys.

I have often thought of those touching appellations which are given to the Great Supreme, especially in the relation he sustains to the sons and daughters of sorrow. The apostle Paul speaks of him as "THE GOD OF CONSOLATION; elsewhere he speaks of him as the God of ALL comfort. He is styled the WIDOW'S HUSBAND AND DEFENDER, and the FATHER OF THE FATHERLESS. He is revealed in the New Testament as the Comforter, and as though there were no other. Under his wise and gracious administration, suffering becomes the parent of joy– the wife loses her husband, that she may have God for her portion and guide; the parent loses his child, that he may have God for his Father; the rich lose their wealth, that the living God may be their portion; the ambitious and aspiring lose their honors, that He may be "their glory, and the lifter up of their head."

When the celebrated Dr. Samuel Johnson was called to follow a beloved wife to the grave, though no preacher of the gospel, he wrote her funeral-sermon. Among many excellent thoughts in this discourse, he says, "To afford adequate consolation to the last hour, to cheer the gloomy passage through the valley of the shadow of death, and to ease that anxiety to which beings anticipation of their own dissolution, and conscious of their own danger, must be necessarily exposed, is the privilege only of the Christian religion. To bring life and immortality to light, to give such proofs of our future existence as may influence the most narrow mind and fill the most capacious intellect, to open prospects beyond the grave in which thought may expatiate without obstruction, and to supply a refuge and support to the mind amid all the miseries of decaying nature, is the peculiar excellence of the gospel of Christ. Without this heavenly instructor, he who feels himself sinking under the weight of years, or melting away by the slow waste of lingering disease, has no other remedy than obdurate patience, a gloomy resignation to that which cannot be avoided." The time will come when the wise as well as the unwise will appreciate this great truth, and when "everyone who thirsts" will draw water from these wells of salvation.

In Christian lands the mission of sorrow and the mission of the gospel stand abreast. Christian ministers, like their divine Lord, are ministers of mercy. Their observation and their testimony come to us from the chambers of sickness and the house of mourning. And what are they? "I have seen," said a departed man of God, not many years ago the adornment of the American pulpit, "I have seen this Gospel hush into a calm the tempest raised in the bosom by conscious guilt. I have seen it melt down the most obdurate into tenderness and contrition. I have seen it cheer up the broken-hearted, and bring the tear of gladness into eyes swollen with grief. I have seen it produce and maintain serenity under evils which drive the worldling mad. I have seen it reconcile the sufferer to his cross, and send the song of praise from lips quivering with agony. I have seen it enable the most affectionate relatives to part in death; not without emotion, but without repining, and with a cordial surrender of all they held most dear, to the disposal of their heavenly Father. I have seen the fading eye brighten at the promise of Jesus, 'Where I am, there shall my servant be.' I have seen the faithful spirit released from its clay, now mildly, now triumphantly, to enter into the joy of its Lord." In all the pages of human philosophy, where are to be found consolations like these?

Affliction is also the best expositor of God's word. No small part of it is especially addressed to the children of sorrow. To a sufferer languishing on the couch of debility and pain– to a mourner depressed and desolate under crushing bereavements, there are no themes of contemplation so well timed and welcome, nor any so fitted to heal the heart already bruised, to tenderness– as these precious counsels of heavenly love. It is the voice of heaven, even though it comes on the cold night air, or the bloody battlefield, or the engulfing ocean, or the poisoned atmosphere. It is like the angel messenger in the Garden.

The children of sorrow are sensitive; their minds are easily arrested by God's truth; they read it, they hear it, they turn it over in their thoughts as they are not used to do in the days of cheerfulness and mirth. Martin Luther says "he never understood the book of Psalms until he was in trouble." Again he says, "It was tribulation made me understand the Bible." Its richness, its beauty, its power are more than ever then seen and felt. We more than believe it; we know it, we feel it; it is in-wrought in our experience. We listen with gratified earnestness and grateful emotion to its promises, as though they were something new.

Who but the child of sorrow ever appreciated the beauty and force of such cheering words as the following– "When the poor and needy seek water, and there is none, and their tongue fails for thirst, I the Lord will hear them, I the God of Israel will not forsake them." Creatures are broken cisterns, that hold no water. The mourner wearies in his search; his tongue fails for thirst, until he finds rivers opened even on the sandy and barren places of his pilgrimage, and enjoys in the desert, the cedar and the myrtle and the fig-tree and the pine and the palm tree together. How many millions of God's afflicted ones have hailed the light of that comprehensive and cheering promise– "But now, O Israel, the Lord who created you says– Do not be afraid, for I have ransomed you. I have called you by name; you are mine. When you go through deep waters and great trouble, I will be with you. When you go through rivers of difficulty, you will not drown! When you walk through the fire of oppression, you will not be burned up; the flames will not consume you. For I am the Lord, your God, the Holy One of Israel, your Savior."

Oh, it is like the moon "walking in her brightness" through a night of storms. "The Spirit of the Sovereign Lord is upon me," says the promised Messiah, "because the Lord has appointed me to bring good news to the poor. He has sent me to comfort the brokenhearted and to announce that captives will be released and prisoners will be freed. He has sent me to tell those who mourn that the time of the Lord's favor has come, and with it, the day of God's anger against their enemies. To all who mourn in Israel, he will give beauty for ashes, joy instead of mourning, praise instead of despair. For the Lord has planted them like strong and graceful oaks for his own glory." Isaiah 61:1-3

There is no book like the Bible in the time of trial. "Blessed is the man," says the Psalmist, "whom you chasten, O Lord, and teach him out of your word." God's truth is unchanging and eternal. Once planted in the soul, it shall bring forth fruit. One lesson truly learned from it, and that would not have been otherwise learned, is worth all our tears. It was no undue estimate of it that led one of old to say, "Unless your law had been my delight, I should have perished in my affliction. Trouble and anguish have taken hold on me; yet your commandments are my delight." I pity the man who, in the day of trial, is ignorant of the Bible. The bright and permanent realities of God's truth are alone able to cheer him. In every view this book of God is a most wonderful book. To an afflicted man it occupies a place which no other can occupy. Only infinite wisdom and infinite love could have made it what it is. Human wisdom has no part in it. It shines by its own light, is hallowed by its own sanctity, embalmed in its own love. It is sorrow's "silent comforter."

> "There no delusive hope invites despair;
> No mockery meets you, no delusion there;
> The spells and charms that blinded you before,
> All vanish there and fascinate no more."

There is a voice from that new-made grave saying to those who mourn– prize these messages of heavenly wisdom and tenderness. They come from the "spirit-land." However bitter your cup, you will not faint in the day of adversity, so long as the Bible is the more precious for all that you suffer. Fly from gloom and sadness to God's word. Fly from the darts of the fowler to his word; and though you will find there everything to instruct and much to reprove you, you will there find that "all things work together for good to those who love God, and are the called according to his purpose."

SORROW AT THE THRONE OF GRACE

"Is any among you afflicted? let him pray."

We cannot misunderstand nor misinterpret this apostolic injunction, nor doubt as to those to whom it is definitely addressed. Are there those who are suffering from poverty? They are the afflicted. Poverty, dependence, and mortification are a bitter cup to the proud and selfish heart. To be cast upon the cold charities of this heartless world, is to be a man of sorrows. Are there those who are suffering from the neglect or contempt of others? They are the afflicted. Their sorrows may never be told, but remain shut up within their own bosoms; but they are sad and depressing sorrows. Are there those who suffer from oppression and wrong? They are the afflicted. Such were the afflictions of the psalmist when Ahithophel deserted and Shimei cursed him, and Saul and Absalom thirsted for his blood. Are there those who suffer from unjust imputations and false invective? They are the afflicted. To an honorable mind, no trial is more severe than the pestilential breath of calumny and reproach. Are there those who suffer from disappointments and losses? They are the afflicted. "The rich man fades away in his ways." His property is lost on the ocean, or destroyed by fire, or injured by accident, or torn from him by dishonesty and fraud; and he feels the loss. Are there those who suffer from trying bereavements? They are the afflicted. God has removed the desire of their eyes with a stroke; lover and friend are taken away, and their acquaintance, into darkness. Man goes to his long home, and the mourners go about the streets. Are there those who suffer from pain and sickness? They are the afflicted. "In the morning they say, would to God it were evening; and in the evening, would to God it were morning." They are "made to possess months of vanity, and wearisome nights are appointed unto them."

Afflictions like these crave alleviation. What shall it be? You cannot relieve the poverty of the poor, nor reverse the sentence of neglect and contempt, nor arrest the arm of oppression and cruelty, nor seal the lips of the calumniator, nor recompense the losses of the unfortunate, nor bring back the departed from the tomb, nor heal the maladies of the body or mind. It is no comfort to counsel these children of sorrow, that since it is their allotment to suffer, it must be their allotment to endure. Endurance does not relieve one pang, and only abandons the hope of relief. You may counsel them to forget their trials; but memory cannot bid sorrow be gone, so long as the heart bleeds. You may counsel them to drown their sorrows in the cares of the world, and by a resort to its mirthful companions and fashionable amusements. But miserable, miserable comforters are they all.

The afflicted must look higher than the world. They must look away beyond the everlasting hills whence comes their help. The children of sorrow feel their helplessness; nor is there any such relief as that which is found at the throne of heavenly grace. Let them bear their sorrows to the closet, to the family altar, and to the sanctuary. If you have hitherto lived a prayerless life, let your afflictions urge you to pray, and instruct you to come to the throne to obtain mercy, and find grace to help in the time of need. If you are a man of prayer, let your afflictions urge you to retire from the world, and to be much alone with God. You will learn there to know more of him, to love him more, and trust him more. Your murmuring heart will learn to be still there; you will lay your hand upon your mouth, and say, "Behold, I am vile; what shall I answer you?"

The world little knows the satisfaction which the children of sorrow enjoy, when in the exercise of a filial spirit, and by a living faith in the great Mediator, they hold communion with God, and come near, even to his seat, and fill their mouth with arguments. They repair then to the Being who can remove or sanctify their sorrows. He said to the father of the faithful, "I am the Almighty God– fear not; I am your shield, and your exceeding great reward." He is the God of creation, of providence, and of grace. He can avert the sorrows they feel. He can lift the needy from the ash-heap, and set him among princes. He can extort from their enemies the tribute of affection and homage. He can cover them with his feathers, and under his wings they shall trust. He can hide them in the secret of his presence from the pride of man. He can keep them secretly in a position from the strife of tongues. He can rebuke the devourer for their sakes, and give them a name and a place better than that of sons or of daughters. He can bid the destroyer put up his sword into its scabbard. In every instance he will remove the afflictions of the suppliant where it is best for him that they should be removed. And where he does not see fit to remove them, he will make them the means of a more progressive holiness and spiritual comfort. His grace shall be sufficient for these children of sorrow, teaching them by this beneficial discipline to live above the world and walk with God. Afflictions are to the soul what storms and frost are to the earth. For a while they deform the face of nature; they tell us of its solitude and barrenness and desertion; and it feels like winter as we pass over its fields;

but they prepare the soil for the verdure and promise of the harvest.

This near communion with God is also the direct way to remove from his people the cause of their afflictions. As we have already seen, they are like the refiner's crucible. Mourners who never pray, instead of being made better by their sorrows, are made worse. Like Pharaoh, they harden their hearts, and become insolent and rebellious. In the day of their adversity, they sin faster and stronger than ever. But it is not so with those who, in the time of their tribulation, enter into their chambers and shut the doors behind them. They find not only a better mind under their afflictions, but present comfort and support. These God alone is able to impart, and will impart to those who seek his face. It is a sweet thought, that there is one gracious Being who has access to the mind, even when the body is enervated by the debility, or racked by the torture of disease. Sorrow has a heart of exquisite tenderness– a heart whose thousand chords yield harmony or loose discord, as they are touched by human hands or divine.

"No wounds like those a wounded spirit feels;
No cure for such until God, who makes them, heals."

He alone can support and cheer the soul when blasted by the storm and stung by the arrows of adversity. His still small voice reaches the sufferer's ear in the dungeon, and soothes his fears in the burning, fiery furnace. "The name of the Lord is a strong tower, into which the righteous runs, and is safe." When the fountains of the great deep are broken up, and the windows of heaven are opened, they are safely embosomed in the ark. There stands the promise– "Call upon me in the day of trouble; I will deliver you, and you shall glorify me." The afflicted have trusted in God, and in so doing have never been confounded. When the atrocious Herod beheaded John the Baptist, the disciples took up the body and buried it, and "went and told Jesus." When the women at the sepulcher trembled, a voice came to them, saying, "Be not affrighted; you seek Jesus, who was crucified." When the exiled disciple fell down as one dead before the overwhelming glory of his divine Lord, the Savior said to him, "Fear not; I am the first and the last– I am he who lives, and was dead; and behold, I am alive for evermore; and have the keys of hell and of death." The sorrows of the bereaved are not spread before Jesus in vain. No being in the universe has a deeper sympathy with them; "in all their afflictions he is afflicted; the angel of his presence saved them; in his love and in his pity he redeemed them." When he was on the earth, the poor, the sorrowing, and the miserable everywhere sent forth the cry, "Have mercy on us, O Lord." He "had compassion on the multitude;" he "had compassion" on the man possessed with devils; he "had compassion" on the widow of Nain. He invites all "who labor and are heavy-laden" to come to him and find rest. There is no cloud so dark but the light of his countenance can turn the shadow of death into the morning, and no mourning so sad but he can give songs in the night. He does more than pity; he turns their mourning into joy. This is his character, this is his office; and though now exalted at the right hand of God, it is that he may "comfort all that mourn."

It is the mission of sorrow therefore to take the mourner by the hand, and lead him to the throne of heavenly grace. There the afflicted find consolation; there "a portion shall be given unto six, yes, unto seven." Behold, he prays, is the precursor of the divine presence. There are tokens of the divine favor which come only by prayer. Cheering, most cheering are those beams of the Sun of righteousness which thus fall upon the gloom and solitude of adversity. These sharp distresses would be overwhelming but for free access to the Hearer of prayer. We can bear them, if God is with us. But if we have no faith nor hope in God– if all our resources are within ourselves, and all our refuge in this perishing world, and we have no access to the Father of mercies and God of all comfort– this is to have no hope, and to be without God in the world.

Every prayerless man is thus ungodly, thus hopeless-- ungodly and hopeless even in prosperity, much more in adversity. His path lies through a world of sorrow; he is an orphan, and has no comforter. If those sorrows do but make you a man of prayer, you will make them welcome. We say then again, in the words of the apostle, "Is any among you afflicted? let him pray." Whatever be his conflicts or his trials--let him pray. Let him ask for anything, for everything he needs. "Open your mouth wide, and I will fill it. Ask, and it shall be given you. I am God," all-sufficient. Go to him daily, and live on his fullness. The greater your trials--the more ready is he to hear; the greater your needs-- the more ready is he to give. You cannot ask too much, you cannot hope too much from God. You cannot measure his munificence; it is a boundless ocean, supplying the greatest needs as easily as the least. The greater the blessing, the more is he gratified with the giving. Go with the spirit of prayer, and you shall meet with no chilling repulse. Though a woman forgets her nursing child, God will not, in the time of their tribulation, forget his mourners.

> "I seem forsaken and alone,
> I hear the tempest roar,
> And every door is shut but one,
> And that is mercy's door."

FITNESS FOR HEAVEN THROUGH SORROW

God's people are dear to him. They are his because
they are his creatures. He made them, and he made them
"for himself." "The Lord, he is God; he has made us, and
not we ourselves." Before he formed them, they were
nothing. Just as "the sea is his," because "he made it;" just
as the heavens are his, and the earth also is his, and the
world and the fullness thereof are his, because he has
founded them, so his people are his, because he called them
into existence. "O Jacob and Israel, you are my servant– I
have formed you; you are my servant." His people are his
absolute, inalienable property by this original and
independent right of creation. They are and ever have been
the objects of his preserving, watchful, and paternal care.
His Son has redeemed them; they were given to him by his
Father, and he bought them by his own precious blood.

"They shall be mine, says the Lord, in the day that I
make up my jewels." They are his peculiar treasure, vessels
of mercy and honor, and their names are all recorded in
"the Lamb's book of life." They are "lovely through the
loveliness he puts upon them;" a "crown of glory in the
hand of the Lord, and a royal diadem in the hand of our
God," and are destined to shine in his own kingdom forever
and ever. Yet by nature they are very unfitted for this high
destiny. They scarcely thought of God, and never loved
him. They cast off fear, and restrained prayer, and rebelled
against him, though he nourished and brought them up as
children.

There is a wide difference between a man who is born
in sin, and the same man who dies a Christian. The first
thing, in order to fit him for heaven, is that a work of grace
should be begun in his heart. There has been a movement

in heaven towards him. "We love Him because he first loved us." God himself is the author and finisher of man's redemption. There is the work which Jesus Christ has performed for his people, and there is the work which the Holy Spirit performs in them. The work performed outside them has its counterpart in the work performed within them. God himself alone has the power to change their hearts, to form them new creatures, to make them vessels of mercy, to turn them from darkness to light, and from the power of Satan to the liberty with which Christ makes them free. "To as many as received him, to them gave he power to become the sons of God, even to those who believe on his name; who were born, not of blood, nor of the will of the flesh, nor of the will of man, but of God." None are fitted for heaven unless their hearts are thus turned from sin to holiness, and receive this hallowed and heavenward direction and tendency. "Verily, I say unto you, Except a man be born again, he cannot see the kingdom of God." This is an important epoch in the history of every redeemed sinner, and the first effectual step in preparing him for heaven.

This work of grace must also be carried on; and he who "began it will perform it until the day of Jesus Christ." Support in the time of need is outside of themselves. If they are not overcome in the spiritual warfare, it is because the Captain of their salvation watches over them, cares for them, and throws around them the shield of his salvation. "In them, that is, in their flesh, there dwells no good thing." They are exposed to wander, to backslide, to plunge into fatal snares; nor would they ever return if he did not reclaim them; nor would they ever reach the celestial city if he did not "restore their souls, and lead them in paths of righteousness for his name's sake."

In making his people fit for the inheritance of the saints in light, the God of all grace, as has already been remarked, makes use of his word and ordinances. And it is when afflictive dispensations run through and are intermingled with the means of grace and salvation, that they ordinarily enjoy heart-affecting views of invisible and eternal realities. Seasons of trial become seasons of divine manifestation.

God is pleased to manifest himself to them as he does not to the world. As such views are not essential to a state of grace, God gives them as their peculiar circumstances require. They are precious manifestations in the hour of trial; they leave lasting impressions on the mind, and are never forgotten. Sometimes they come upon them unexpected, and almost unsought– it may be in the darkest night of their sorrow, and when they feel most like pilgrims and strangers on the earth, and are most oppressed by the solitude of the wilderness. The saddest hours are often cheered by the most hallowed themes. Hallowed moments of celestial visitation are they when faith, with more than ordinary vividness, realizes the unseen world; and hope, full of immortality, sheds its fragrance over the soul and makes it long for heaven.

It is true that seasons of affliction are not always thus favored. They are sometimes seasons of darkness and sore temptation, as Christian biography teaches us. "Alas," said Lady Russel, when her noble husband was sent to the block by the licentious and inexorable Charles, "I want liberty to approach nearer my heavenly Friend. But my understanding is clouded, my faith weak, sense strong, and Satan busy in filling my thoughts with false notions, difficulties, and doubts respecting a future state and the efficacy of prayer. My thoughts fly everywhere but to

God." This is a most unhappy state of mind; but it is by no means of so frequent occurrence as those bright views which discover the pillar of cloud by day and of fire by night.

The early Christians were remarkable examples of this hallowed influence of trials. They "gloried in tribulation," because it was the means of sustaining a heavenward tendency of mind. They looked upon it as a privilege to suffer. "Unto you it is given in the behalf of Christ, not only to believe on his name, but to suffer for his sake." Strange as it may appear to us, faith and suffering are both declared to be the gift of God. Such was the apostle Paul's love to his divine Master, that he could affirm, "I take pleasure in infirmities, in reproaches, in necessities, in persecutions, in distresses for Christ's sake."

These primitive disciples of the New Testament were the noblest of men. Their habitual language was, "For our light affliction, which is for a moment, works for us a far more exceeding and eternal weight of glory; while we look not at the things that are seen; but at the things that are unseen." Their character was formed and developed by the severe discipline of adversity. Trials indicated their sincerity, proved the strength of their faith and the strength of their consolations, and gave brilliancy to the crown of their rejoicing. They were not more partakers in the sufferings of Christ, than they are the partakers in his glory. "We are joint-heirs with Christ," say they, "if so be that we suffer with him, that we may be glorified together." They "reckoned that the sufferings of this present time are not worthy to be compared with the glory which shall be revealed."

If we ever get to heaven, we shall see that it was not our own wisdom or fidelity that brought us there. Every step we have taken would have been a false one, but for God. He moved first, and we did but follow as fast and as far as he drew us and led the way. Of all the events and circumstances which were either in themselves auspicious to our salvation or overruled to our spiritual welfare, our trials will never be forgotten. Thousands upon thousands have been made fit for heaven by their trials. The fetters of gold which bound them to earth have been thus sundered, and even the ties of nature have been held by a looser hand. They would not live always, but desired rather to depart and be with Christ. This world does not compensate for the sorrow and pain and conflict and sin of living in it beyond the bounds of our appointed time. True Christians have more and better friends in heaven than they have on earth, and who wait to give them a joyful greeting. It is no marvel that they sometimes "struggle and pant to be free," and long to "put on their blood-bought attire," and "wonder and worship" with those who, like themselves, are "washed, and justified, and sanctified in the name of the Lord Jesus, and by the Spirit of our God."

How many, do you think, are now in heaven who bless God even for the bitterest cup? How many can say, "I dallied with sin and trifled with the Tempter; I picked flowers on the brink of the precipice, but found a gravestone there which told me of one I loved. I had gone astray, but my grief agitated me, my depression humbled me, my sins alarmed me. My idol was there, and my heart bled. I thought of death and eternity, and was separated from them only by the breath of my nostrils. God smote me, but he made all my bed in my sickness. I was afraid to die, but when I came to the conflict, I found the foe vanquished. Death was swallowed up in victory. It is all reality now, all heaven, all joy, all praise to God my Redeemer, God all-sufficient, God all in all."

Sanctified afflictions will not be forgotten in heaven. "You shall remember all the way your God led you in the wilderness." To suffer God's will is as truly honorable to him and profitable to our own spiritual interests--as to do his will. They are equally acts of obedience. When sufferings are endured with a Christian spirit and wisely employed, not only is the work of God thereby manifested in the sufferers, but their own future blessedness is thereby promoted. If they were not always happy in their trials, they will be happy in their triumphs, happy in their eternal home.

When the exiled apostle was in Patmos, one of the elders before the throne said to him, "Who are these that are arrayed in white robes, and whence come they?" The apostle was unable to answer the question, and replied, "Sir, you know." "These are those," said the angelic messenger, "who have come out of the great tribulation; they have washed their robes and made them white in the blood of the Lamb. Therefore, they are before the throne of God and serve him day and night in his temple; and he who sits on the throne will spread his tent over them. Never again will they hunger; never again will they thirst. The sun will not beat upon them, nor any scorching heat. For the Lamb at the center of the throne will be their shepherd; he will lead them to springs of living water. And God will wipe away every tear from their eyes."

The most afflicted and desolate will then prove the love and faithfulness of the severest chastisements. "There remains a rest for the people of God," a perfect and everlasting rest. If by marvelous grace in Christ Jesus you ever enter it, you will look back with grateful admiration at the tender care and covenant faithfulness of Him who loved you. And as you look back and call to mind how often you grieved his Spirit and forfeited his love, and how, but for these desolating afflictions, you never would have entered the heavenly city, you may well say with dear Richard Baxter, "When he broke your heart, as well as when he bound it up, your blessed Redeemer was saving you." With adoring surprise you may exclaim with him, "O blessed way, and thrice-blessed end! Is my mourning and my heavy walking come to this? Are all my afflictions come to this? Blessed gales--which have blown me into such a harbor! Oh what a God there is in heaven!"

Such is the mission of sorrow. Its lessons cannot be learned from the teachings of human wisdom.

It may be you have been thrown upon a bed of sickness, and even painful and lingering agony. The bloom of health fades on your cheek, and wasting debility warns you of the grave. God grant that celestial visions may throng around your pillow, and that underneath that aching head you may find the everlasting arms. It may be "a wife of youth" has sunk to the grave, and the heart that watched her lingering decay, amid its alternate hopes and fears, sinks under the blow. And can you not lean on an almighty arm, and make your refuge in the shadow of his wings?

Perhaps you have seen a favorite child sinking under a disease that was appointed to do its fatal work. You have turned from the scene with sighing. Your fears have been realized. The flower is cut down, and withers in the grave. Mourning parent, strive to look upward. It may cost you tears; but God would teach you that his favor, without earthly comforts, is worth more to you than all earthly

comforts without his favor. He sent this crushing calamity
on purpose to throw a temporary cloud over the sun of
time, and open to you the brighter scenes of a sinless world.
He would cement, rather than sunder the bond that unites
you to the departed. That bright spirit has left you, and your
fondest, proudest wishes– dust is upon them. These
sorrows have their mission.

> "Your God, to call you homeward,
> His only Son sent down;
> And now, still more to tempt your heart,
> Has taken up your own."

Of such is the kingdom of heaven. Your jewel shines
in your Redeemer's crown. Would you pluck that little star
from his brow? If you could, would you call back the
beloved one?

O you who weep and you who have wept, you who are
far from God and you who are brought near, come and
learn from him the sweet supports of his truth and grace in
the hour of trial, and the precious lessons which his Spirit
inculcates in the school of affliction. Sorrow is the sad
heritage of sin. Let it soften your heart and render it more
susceptible to the influences of heavenly grace. Bow under
these strokes of the rod, and then lift your eyes to the hills
whence comes your help. Mourning friends, though "you
walk in the midst of trouble, God will revive you. Though
he causes grief, yet will he have compassion, according to
the multitude of his mercies." These exhausting days and
wearisome nights will soon be over. The aching head, the
throbbing heart will before long be at rest. God's voice to
you is, "For a small moment have I forsaken you, but with
great mercies will I gather you; in a little wrath I hid my

face from you for a moment, but with everlasting kindness
will I have mercy on you, says the Lord your Redeemer."

"The path of sorrow, and that path alone,
Leads to the land where sorrow is unknown;
No traveler ever reached that blessed abode,
Who found not thorns and briars on his road."

NO SORROW THERE

In heaven at last. The days of mourning are ended.
God shall wipe away all tears from their eyes. To the
wicked he says, "Woe unto you who laugh now; for you
shall mourn and weep," to the righteous, "Blessed are you
who weep now; for you shall laugh." Everlasting joy shall
be upon their head, and sorrow and sighing shall flee away.

"O blessed way, and thrice-blessed end!" We are still
in the wilderness, and have not yet reached that city of our
God. We are still buffeting the storm, but pressing onward
to the land where clouds and darkness are known no more.

The soul of man in the present world is no true
expression of its Maker's handiwork. Its elements are
incongruous and discordant. It is a disjointed mechanism;
unrefined and undirected, all its movements are ominous of
disaster. It needs to pass through the furnace, before it shall
come out in purity and brightness. So long as the people of
God linger on these shores of time, they will not only be
suffering, but sinning men. "I shall be satisfied," says the
Psalmist, "when I awake in your likeness." Nothing else
satisfies. The regenerated soul thirsts for God, for the living
God. The turbid and bitter waters of earth have served to
prepare it for the pure river of life. Nor was the process

completed until, at the grave's mouth, the last chain that bound it to earth was dissolved. These infirmities and sins and sorrows will vanish then. Christ's sorrowing followers are made like unto the angels; they are "the children of God, being the children of the resurrection."

Eye has not seen, nor ear heard, nor have entered into the heart of man--the things which God has prepared for those who love him. That is a wondrous world of which the Savior says, "Where I am, there also shall my servant be." It has no need of the sun or the moon to shine in it. The glory and honor of the nations are gathered into it; there is no more curse; but the throne of God and the Lamb shall be in it, and his servants shall serve him. The actual transition of the immortal spirit from time to eternity, from earth to heaven, no human eye ever beheld. No ear of man ever heard the shout, as the weary feet of the once mourning pilgrim were first planted on the long wished for shore, though guardian angels hovered over him as he passed through the dark valley.

There is no darkness now; the Lamb is the light thereof; they are the dazzling glories of eternal day. When the martyr Stephen fell, he exclaimed, "I see the glory of God, and Jesus standing at the right hand of God." And what must be the vision when the children of sorrow see him face to face, and know even as they are known; where "the ransomed of the Lord return, and come to Zion with songs and everlasting joy upon their heads, and they shall obtain joy and gladness, and sorrow and sighing shall flee away."

Well may they look to the rock whence they were hewn, and the hole of the pit whence they were dug. It was a world alienated from God, and where sorrow upon sorrow, and convulsion upon convulsion agitated it in a thousand forms. It is a mournful, a fearful retrospect they look upon, with only here and there a few radiations – Is this the dark land from which we have been rescued, and this the wilderness we have traveled over?

And how were they rescued? They were partakers in the universal apostasy, and under the condemning sentence of that law which is holy, just, and good. It was not by works of righteousness which they had done, or ever could perform. They are redeemed sinners, and would have sunk under the weight of their iniquity, had not the God-man bore their sins in his own body on the tree. Not a thread, not a filament, not a fiber of their justifying righteousness was wrought by their own hands. And their personal holiness, whence was it? Who made them to differ from a world that lies in wickedness--and from what they themselves once were? When days of trial came, and temptations assaulted them, and flesh and sense were arrayed against them; when there was conflict and tumult, and the subtle adversary went about seeking whom he might devour; who stimulated them to watch and pray, and wrestle and overcome? Whose unsleeping eye and unwearied arm and unchanging faithfulness cared for them in youth, in manhood, and in old age– at home and abroad, in health and in sickness, in storm and in sunshine? And whose were those everlasting arms ever and anon thrown around them; and whose that loving heart, giving them the oil of joy for mourning, and the garment of praise for the spirit of heaviness, lest they should be discouraged in the conflict, and never reach the heavenly land?

Many a youthful pilgrim who seemed to run well, grew weary and fainted, and turned back. The wilderness, as they look back upon it, is strewed with the fainting, the slumbering, the fallen, the dead, the lost. From the cradle to the grave, and from the grave up to the heavenly city, every incident in their history, every joy and every pang of sorrow has been under the control of infinite love. Even the hairs of their head were all numbered. Will it not be delightful to look back and see how the outstretched arm was spread over them, and how they were borne as on eagles' wings?

Oh what adoring, what humble thankfulness will then take the place of that restless and depressed and murmuring spirit with which they so unsubmissively endured their trials in the present world. Sweet reminiscences these, that make the mourner humble. Blessed retrospect, that prostrates the soul in the dust, and makes it fall at the feet of Jesus, and cover its angelic face with its wings. Profound will be the veneration with which they enter into his presence and contemplate his awesome majesty, yet calm and tranquil as the sea of glass on which they stand to show forth his praise. Never will they again love the creature more than the Creator. They are lost and swallowed up, not in the floods of earthly sorrow, but the ocean of heavenly joy– not in themselves and those they loved on the earth, but in the uncreated, undying glories of the Infinite One. It will be the wonder of their eternity that they are thus filled with all the fullness of God, and that, plunging as they once were in miry places, they now float in that ocean of light and love where there is neither bottom nor shore!

The humility of heaven is one of the brightest features of its character, and one of the sources of its sweetest joy. Honors they have; but they cast their crowns before the throne. If "pride was not made for man," it will never be found in heaven. Its empire on earth is world-wide and powerful; it reigns in hell; but in the spirits of just men made perfect, it shall find no place. Amid the splendors of that everlasting and glorious world, every laurel withers that is not wreathed around the Savior's brow. If the religion of earth is the religion of heaven in miniature, the purest gem that adorns it is this heaven-born humility. It is a sacred thing, because it is so humble and lies so low. We should love to think of that blessed world if it were only for its humility. When those ransomed spirits, weary of the conflicts of earth, repose under the shadow of the tree of life, and there, at the feet of the enthroned Lamb, reflect upon the way they have been led through the wilderness, and look down upon the agonies of that eternal pit from which they have been rescued, how can it be otherwise than that a deep and everlasting sense of their unworthiness and ill-desert should add to the fullness of their gratitude and joy?

They are perfectly humble, and perfectly happy. From the hour of their conversion, redeeming love has been their theme; but never until now, as they stand on Mount Zion, have they given utterance to the ecstasy of their joy. And even here, on this low earth, where the graves of the departed are scattered and the cypress mourns, voices are not lacking, embarrassed and suppressed it may be by their tears, to utter the song, "You are worthy; for you were slain, and have redeemed us unto God by your blood." Oh that I could direct the eyes of the mourner upward, and in these hours of darkness bid his heart rest on that blessed world where, in a few short hours, all, both among the living and the dead, who fear God and love his Son, will meet in holier and more intimate fellowship. "Up there," sin and sorrow and death never enter. "Up there," sighs and farewells are a sound unknown. "Up there," they sit together in heavenly places, and drink the wine new with Christ in his Father's kingdom. "Up there," the holy men and women who parted at the grave, redeemed parents and their redeemed children, whom the voice of the archangel and the trumpet of God have summoned from the sleep of centuries, will meet, not to recount their own sorrows, but to tell of him who came to the humiliation of the manger, and the agonies of the cross--to rescue them from endless weeping and infinite despair!

"I heard a loud shout from the throne, saying, "Look, the home of God is now among his people! He will live with them, and they will be his people. God himself will be with them. He will remove all of their sorrows, and there will be no more death or sorrow or crying or pain. For the old world and its evils are gone forever." And the one sitting on the throne said, "Look, I am making all things new!" And then he said to me, "Write this down, for what I tell you is trustworthy and true." Revelation 21:3-5.

Made in the USA
Monee, IL
06 December 2024

72728218R00039